POPE
JOHN PAUL II

*The Things
of the Spirit*

POPE
JOHN PAUL II

*The Things
of the Spirit*

*edited by
Kathryn Spink*

1817

HARPER & ROW, PUBLISHERS, SAN FRANCISCO
*Cambridge, Hagerstown, New York, Philadelphia
London, Mexico City, São Paulo, Sydney*

In addition to extracts from recordings made by the editor
during papal visits to Ireland and the United States, the
publisher gratefully acknowledges the inclusion of excerpts
from transcripts in *L'Osservatore Romano*.

FIRST U.S. EDITION

Designed by Donna Davis

Library of Congress Cataloging in Publication Data

John Paul II, Pope, 1920-
    THE THINGS OF THE SPIRIT
    1. Christian life—Catholic authors. 2. Church and social
problems—Catholic Church. 3. Catholic Church—Doctrinal
and controversial works—Catholic authors.
I. Spink, Kathryn.   II. Title.
BX2350.2.J637   1982   248.4'82   82-47793
ISBN 0-06-064185-1

82   83   84   85   86   10   9   8   7   6   5   4   3   2   1

CONTENTS

One of the temptations of the modern world is a growing materialism in the outlook of people and of society itself. Many people have been deceived in this regard; they have been led to think that money, pleasure, comfort or self-indulgence can be substitutes for spiritual values.

So, I invite all of you not to lose sight of the things that really matter, the things of the spirit; and let us remember, above all, that it is God who gives meaning to our lives.

To all of you, young and old, I say, do not let the material things of life rob you of the things that really count: God's love for you, and your love for one another.

INTRODUCTION

W hen, at the conclusion of the conclave of October 1978, white smoke finally rose from the flue above St. Peter's
Square, it was to announce to an astonished world the emergence of the first
non-Italian Pope in 450 years. Inevitably,
as news of a new era in the history of the
papacy spread, the flood of congratula-
tions was accompanied by eager specu-
lation as to the thinking behind the
choice of a Polish Cardinal whose name,
Karol Wojtyla, was as yet unfamiliar to
the general public outside Poland.

Yet, surprising as the result of the conclave was to the world at large, the election of Pope John Paul II was by no means inexplicable, not least because his active part in the Second Vatican Council and his membership in the Synod of Bishops had brought him into contact with the broad arena of the "International Church" and earned him a reputation as an outstanding theologian. As a young bishop he had made a significant contribution to the shaping of the Council's important documents. In Lumen Gentium (the Dogmatic Constitution of the Church) and Gaudium et Spes (the Pastoral Constitution on the Church in the Modern World), he had been primarily concerned with developing the theology of the lay apostolate; in 1974 as a leading figure in the international Synod of Bishops, he had contributed an important paper on the theology of evangelization. He was known to be a man of intellect: a linguist who spoke Italian, English, Spanish, French, and Russian, and a man whose academic career as a student at the Jagiellonian University in Cracow, at the Pontifical University Angelicum in Rome, and subsequently as Head of Lublin's Institute of Ethics was outstanding. Furthermore, he was a writer whose numerous books on ethics, on family life, and on the implications of the Second Vatican Council had won him international recognition not only as a theologian but also as a man of letters.

Despite its tragic brevity, the thirty-three-day pontificate of Pope John Paul I had been an instructive one for the College of Cardinals. John Paul I had been elected for his pastoral qualities and his ability to communicate with people, and in this respect the Cardinals' choice would appear to have been appropriate.

The smiling Pope with his love for children, the poor, and the third world had certainly drawn the crowds. If the brief interval he had been granted as "supreme pastor" had revealed any weakness, it lay in the direction of political awareness, for the man who had once confided, "I am only a poor man, accustomed to small things and silence," had been, by his own admission, ill-equipped to cope with world affairs. His outstanding strength had been above all else his emphasis on the "integrity of faith, the perfection of Christian life, and the discipline of the Church." According to many, it had been a deep hunger for the nourishment of solid spirituality which had attracted the enthusiastic crowds. The way seemed to be open for a people's Pope, a Pope who was well versed in world affairs, but a Pope who would be strong-minded in his emphasis on the spiritual nature of man and firm in his doctrinal teaching.

Unlike his predecessor, Karol Wojtyla, at fifty-eight the youngest Pope to be elected since Pius IX, was physically robust, a keen sportsman who even as Cardinal of Cracow had disconcerted those unaccustomed to athletic churchmen by taking to the snow-covered slopes of the Tatra mountains on his skis. Also unlike his predecessor, he was politically aware and competent. As a Pole who had played a conciliatory but highly effective role in the delicate relationship between the Roman Catholic Church and the Communist authorities in his homeland, he was ideally equipped to cope with the increasingly ominous threat of Euro-Communism. Yet he was also very much a man of the people—the son of a retired lieutenant in the Polish Army who during the Nazi occupation of Poland had experienced hard manual labor. As a young priest he had thought nothing of taking his place among the laborers in the fields, and even as Archbishop of Cracow he had obstinately refused to allow himself to be "set apart or above."

Above all else, however, he was manifestly a man of prayer and of the Spirit. His faith had been tried and tested at an early age through personal tragedy with the loss of his brother and the father to whom he was devoted, and through all the horrors of the Nazi occupation. His early training for the priesthood had been undertaken secretly in the palace of the Archbishop Metropolitan of Cracow, under the constant threat of discovery and possible death at the hands of the German authorities. His image of the priestly vocation and the degree of faith and commitment it called for was indelibly influenced by the example of Father Maksymilian Kolbe, who suffered and eventually volunteered to die in an underground cell in Auschwitz, in order that in his capacity as a Roman Catholic priest he could bring comfort to others condemned to suffocate or starve.

Karol Wojtyla came from a land where Roman Catholicism represents a spiritual and patriotic bastion against the Communist vision of Poland. Understandably, as a Church leader the Polish Cardinal was demanding both of himself and of others. He has always recognized unfalteringly the need for fidelity to the mission with which he has been entrusted, placing considerable emphasis on what he calls "the great discipline of the Church." Yet it is above all else love which, he insists, is central to the Christian message. Without love, we are nothing: with love, "the fountain which nourishes and the climate in which we grow," the door to renewal is never closed.

The call to papal authority invariably includes a call to greater love, for Christ repeatedly asks of the successors to St. Peter the same crucial question delivered to Simon Peter: "Do you love me more than others?" In his first address as Pope, John Paul II chose in all humility to respond to that question: "With St. Paul we repeat, 'For the love of Christ constraineth us.' Right from the beginning we wish to see our ministry as a service of love; this will permeate all our actions." In the first few years of his pontificate John Paul II has preached "the discipline of the Church" heralded by his predecessor, with a love remarkable for its courage. He has not been afraid to abandon the trappings of the papacy to meet those for whom he feels so joyously responsible. He has traveled the world to be with "the poor who are unable to travel to meet their Pope," and in each of the places he has visited, he has made it apparent that the crowds who throng to meet him are not merely crowds but collections of individuals, important in their own right. He has laughed with them, prayed with them, and sung with them, and he has suffered in a way which could not fail to speak to the world. Remarkably, he has survived an unprecedented degree of exposure to emerge as a spiritual leader, universally acknowledged even by his critics to be a "good man," a "man of love," and a powerful witness to his personal commitment to the words of St. Irenaeus: "The glory of God is that man should be fully alive."

Inevitably, John Paul's forthright reassertions of the traditional disciplines of his Church have been criticized and at times even lightly dismissed as the product of a Polish Pope's inability to adjust to the so-called Western secular mentality. Nevertheless, the crowds have continued to cheer as he delivers his theme of "the joy of faith in a troubled world" with clarity, firmness, and unquestionable sincerity. In the United States he condemned the consumerism of one of the world's most affluent societies, and hundreds of thousands of Americans—Catholics and non-Catholics, religious people and atheists—applauded. In Paris he announced that "the Church makes no demands in the domain of sexual morality other than those inseparable from true matrimonial and conjugal love," and 50,000 young people cheered. "Moral permissiveness does not make people happy," he proclaimed, and the applause was tumultuous. Perhaps they cheered these apparently unfashionable points because, in the words of one French journalist, "The Pope has been speaking the language of eternal values, which has not been heard in France for many years." Perhaps too, they cheered because we do not live in an age when the majority of people are excited by the niceties of theological or doctrinal definition but rather in an age when Christianity speaks most meaningfully in the language of active human love and charity.

At the heart of John Paul II's teaching lies the simple but, sadly, frequently overlooked message from the Epistle of St. John: "No man hath seen God at any time. If we love one another, God dwelleth in us, and his love in us." He is speaking out bravely in the cause of the dignity of all men created by God in his own image. The Christian message, he insists, is essentially one of peace, joy, life, and love; in an age when these values are increasingly threatened, we, if we are to become fully human, must not neglect the "things of the spirit." It is to this timeless and universally relevant message that the following extracts from his speeches and homilies bear witness.

Kathryn Spink

If any of our contemporaries do not share the faith and hope which lead me, as a servant of Christ and steward of the mysteries of God, to implore God's mercy for humanity in this hour of history, let them at least try to understand the reason for my concern. It is dictated by love for man, for all that is human.

DIVES IN MISERICORDIA

TAKEN
UP IN
LOVE

❧

The message of love that Christ brought is always important, always relevant. It is not difficult to see how today's world, despite its beauty and grandeur, despite the conquests of science and technology, despite the refined and abundant material goods that it offers, is yearning for more truth, for more love, for more joy.

The progress of humanity must be

measured not only by the progress of science and technology, which shows man's uniqueness with regard to nature, but also and chiefly by the primacy given to spiritual values and the progress of moral life.

Pervading materialism imposes its dominion on everyone today in many different forms and with an aggressiveness that spares no one. The most sacred principles, which were the sure guides for the behavior of individuals and society, are being hollowed out by false pretenses concerning freedom, the sacredness of life, the indissolubility of marriage, the true sense of human sexuality, the right attitude toward the material goods that progress has to offer.

Many people now are tempted to self-indulgence and consumerism, and human identity is often defined by what one owns. Prosperity and affluence, even when they are only beginning to be available to larger strata of society, tend to make people assume that they have a right to all that prosperity can bring, and thus they can become more selfish in their demands. Everybody wants complete freedom in all areas of human behavior, and new models of morality are being proposed in the name of would-be freedom.

When the moral fiber of a nation is weakened, when the sense of personal responsibility is diminished, then the door is open for the justification of injustices, for violence in all its forms, and for the manipulation of the many by the few. The challenge that is already with us is the temptation to accept as true freedom what in reality is only a new form of slavery.

Materialistic concerns and one-sided values are never sufficient to fill the heart and mind of a human person. A life reduced to the sole dimension of possessions, of consumer goods, of temporal concerns will never let you discover and enjoy the full richness of your humanity. It is only in God—in Jesus, God made man—that you will fully understand what you are. He will unveil to you the true greatness of yourselves: that you are redeemed by him and taken up in his love, that you are made truly free in him who said about himself, "If the Son frees you, you will be free indeed.

If Mother Teresa of Calcutta—who is one of those women who, as followers of Christ, are not afraid to descend to all the dimensions of humanity, to all the human situations in the modern world— were present here, she would tell us that along the streets of Calcutta and other cities of the world, people are dying of hunger.

The consumer approach to life does not take into consideration the whole truth about humanity—not the historical truth, nor the social, interior, and metaphysical truth. It is rather a flight from this truth. People are created for happiness, but that happiness is not to be confused with pleasure. Consumer-oriented people lose, in their pursuit of pleasure, the full dimension of their humanity and their awareness of the deepest meaning of life.

"Let the message of Christ, in all its richness, find a home with you." In the knowledge of Christ you have the key to the Gospel. In the knowledge of Christ you have an understanding of the needs of the world. Since he became one with us in all things but sin, your union with Jesus of Nazareth could never, and will never, be an obstacle to understanding and responding to the needs of the world. And finally, in the knowledge of Christ you will not only discover and come to understand the limitations of human wisdom and of human solutions to the needs of humanity, but you will also experience the power of Jesus, and the value of human reason and human endeavor when they are taken up in the strength of Jesus, when they are redeemed by Christ.

Christ is "the way, and the truth, and the life." He put all human life in the true dimension of truth and of authentic love. True knowledge and true freedom are in Jesus. Make Jesus always part of your dedication to the well-being of your fellow human beings.

THE STILL CENTER OF EXISTENCE

⧗

We must find time, we must make time, to be with the Lord in prayer. Following the example of the Lord Jesus himself, we must "always go off to some place where we can be alone and pray." It is only if we spend time with the Lord that our sending out to others will be also a bringing of him to others.

Remember always that your field of apostolate is your own personal lives. Here is where the message of the Gospel has first to be preached and lived. Your first apostolic duty is your own sanctification. No change in religious life has any importance unless it be also movement inwards to the "still center" of your existence, where Christ is. It is not what you do that matters most, but what you are.

In faith we find the victory that overcomes the world. Because we are united with Jesus and sustained by him, there is no challenge we cannot meet, no difficulty we cannot sustain, no obstacle we cannot overcome for the Gospel. Indeed, Christ himself guarantees that "he who believes in me will also do the works that I do; and greater works than these he will do." The answer to so many problems is found only in faith—a faith manifested and sustained in prayer.

Prayer enables us to be converted continually, to remain in a state of continuous reaching out to God, which is essential if we wish to lead others to him. Prayer helps us to believe, to hope, and to love.

Prayer should embrace every part of our life. It cannot be something additional or marginal. Everything should find in prayer its true voice, even the things that burden us, the things of which we are ashamed, the things which by their very nature set us apart from God. Above all, it is prayer that essentially demolishes the barrier which sin and evil may have erected between us and God. Through prayer the whole world must find its proper direction, that is, an orientation toward God: our interior world and also the objective world, the world in which we live, and the world of our experience.

If we are converted to God, then everything in us is directed to him. Prayer is the expression of this being directed to God.

Prayer is the sacrifice of our lips. As St. Ignatius of Antioch writes, it is "spring water that murmurs within us and says: 'Come to the Father.' "

Let your body be in the service of your inner self. Let your gestures, your looks, always be the reflection of your soul.

HOMES
OF
PRAYER

∾

Your homes should always remain homes of prayer.

Modern conditions and social changes have created new patterns and new difficulties for family life and for Christian marriage. I want to say to you: do not be discouraged, do not follow the trends where a close-knit family is seen as outdated. The Christian family is more important for the Church and for society today than ever before.

For each and every family the Pope would like to be able to say a word of encouragement and hope. You families that can enjoy prosperity, do not shut yourselves up in your happiness; open yourselves up to others and distribute what is superfluous for you and what others lack. Families oppressed by poverty, do not lose heart; without making luxury your ideal or riches the principle of happiness, seek with the help of all to overcome difficult moments while waiting for better days. Families visited and tormented by physical or moral pain, sorely tried by sickness or want, do not add bitterness or despair to these sufferings, but temper sorrow with hope.

To you fathers and mothers I say: teach your children how to forgive, make your homes places of love and forgiveness; make your streets and neighborhoods centers of peace and reconciliation. It would be a crime against youth and their future to let even one child grow up with nothing but the experience of violence and hate.

The future of the Church and the future of humanity depend in great part on parents and on the family life they build in their homes. The family is the true measure of the greatness of a nation, just as the dignity of individuals is the true measure of civilization.

It is not without reason that Jesus Christ, the Son of God, spent thirty years of his life hidden at home. He wanted to point out in this way that the home is a power, the fundamental power of man. The family is the historic and visible expression of the love of God, who in his way wished to make people capable of loving and giving their lives, precisely because they are created "in his image and likeness."

The thought that certain ideologies want to destroy the family, spreading alienation and causing disputes, is a sad one. It is sad to think that so many young people leave their own homes, casting their parents into bitterness and despair. That is not the solution. Love your families with generosity, patience, and tact, tolerating those imperfections which no person is without. Make your home an oasis of peace and confidence: pray with your families.

For the Family

Lord God, from you every family in heaven and on earth takes its name. Father, you are love and life.

Through your Son, Jesus Christ, born of woman, and through the Holy Spirit, the fountain of divine charity, grant that every family on earth may become for each successive generation a true shrine of life and love.

Grant that your grace may guide the thoughts and actions of husbands and wives for the good of their families and of all the families in the world.

Grant that the young may find in the family solid support for their human dignity and for their growth in truth and love.

Grant that love, strengthened by the grace of the sacrament of marriage, may prove mightier than all the weaknesses and trials through which our families sometimes pass.

Through the intercession of the Holy Family of Nazareth, grant that the Church may fruitfully carry out her worldwide mission in the family and through the family.

We ask this of you, who is life, truth, and love with the Son and the Holy Spirit. Amen.

THE
EUCHARIST

⚓

From the Upper Room in Jerusalem, from the Last Supper, in a certain sense the Eucharist writes the history of human hearts and of human communities.

It is from the Eucharist that all of us receive the grace and strength for daily living, to live real Christian lives in the joy of knowing that God loves us, that Christ died for us, and that the Holy Spirit lives in us.

Our full participation in the Eucharist is the real source of the Christian spirit that we wish to see in our personal lives and in all aspects of society. Whether we serve in politics, in the economic, cultural, social, or scientific field—no matter what our occupation is—the Eucharist is a challenge to our daily lives.

Dear brothers and sisters, there must always be consistency between what we believe and what we do. We cannot live on the glories of our past Christian history. Our union with Christ in the Eucharist must be expressed in the truth of our lives today—in our action, in our behavior, in our lifestyle, and in our relationship with others. For each one of us the Eucharist is a call to ever greater effort, so that we may live as true followers of Jesus: truthful in our speech, generous in our deeds, concerned, respectful of the dignity and the rights of all persons, whatever their rank or income, self-controlled—looking to the well-being of our families, our young people, our country, the world.

The truth of our union with Jesus Christ in the Eucharist is tested by whether or not we really love our fellow men and women; it is tested by how we treat others, especially our families; husbands and wives, children and parents, brothers and sisters. It is tested by whether or not we forgive those who hurt us or offend us. It is tested by whether we practice in life what our faith teaches us. We must always remember what Jesus said: "You are my friends if you do what I command you."

You cannot be a genuine Christian on Sunday unless you try to be true to

Christ's spirit also in your work, your commercial dealings, at your trade union or your employer's or professional meetings. How can you be a true community in Christ at the Eucharist unless you try to think of the welfare of the whole national community when decisions are being taken by your particular sector or group? How can you be ready to meet Christ in judgment unless you remember how the poor are affected by the behavior of your group or by your personal lifestyle? For Christ will say to us all, "Insofar as you did this to one of the least of these brothers of mine, you did it to me."

THE ROAD
FROM
CHRIST TO
HUMANITY

When we Christians make Jesus Christ the center of our feelings and thoughts, we do not turn away from people and their needs. On the contrary, we are caught up in the eternal movement of God's love that comes to meet us; we are caught up in the movement of the Son, who came among us, who became one of us; we are caught up in the movement of the Holy Spirit, who visits the poor, calms fevered hearts, binds up wounded hearts, warms cold hearts, and gives us the fullness of his gifts. The reason why man is the primary and fundamental way for the Church is that the Church walks in the footsteps of Jesus; it is Jesus who has shown us this road. This road passes in an unchangeable way through the mystery of the Incarnation and Redemption; it leads from Christ to man.

We are in the image of God. We redeem and discover ourselves when we step into this image; when we discover our own likeness to God.

Nothing surpasses the greatness or dignity of a human person. Human life is not just an idea or an abstraction; human life is the concrete reality of a being that lives, that acts, that grows and develops; human life is the concrete reality of a being that is capable of love and of service to humanity.

Human life is precious because it is the gift of a God whose love is infinite; and when God gives life, it is forever.

My own spiritual and religious mission impels me to be the messenger of peace and brotherhood, and to witness to the true greatness of every human person. This greatness derives from the love of God, who created in us his own likeness and gave us an eternal destiny. It is in this dignity of the human person that I see the meaning of history, and that I find the principle that gives sense to the role which every human being has to assume for his or her own advancement and for the well-being of the society to which he or she belongs.

Every time I have the opportunity to meet with a group of people, it gives me great happiness, for in you I see my brothers and sisters, children of the same God, who is our Father, and who has created us with a unique beauty and richness: the great beauty of being free human beings, capable of knowing truth, of offering love and understanding to each other, and of joining hands to make the world a better place in which to live.

When you wonder about the mystery of yourself, look to Christ, who gives you the meaning of life. When you wonder what it means to be a mature person, look to Christ, who is the fullness of humanity, and when you wonder about your role in the future of the world, look to Christ.

THE
POOR
OF THE
WORLD

～

Keep Jesus Christ in your hearts, and you will recognize his face in every human being. You will want to help him out in all his needs, the needs of your brothers and sisters. This is the way we prepare ourselves to meet Jesus, when he will come again on the last day, as the Judge of the living and the dead, and he will say to us: "Come, you have my Father's blessing! Inherit the Kingdom prepared for you from the creation of the world. For I was hungry and you gave me food, I was thirsty and you gave me drink. I was a stranger and you welcomed me, naked and you clothed me. I was ill and you comforted me, in prison and you came to visit me... I assure you as often as you did it for one of my least brethren, you did it for me."

Social thinking and social practice inspired by the Gospel must always be marked by a special sensitivity towards those who are most in distress, those who are extremely poor, those suffering from all the physical, mental, and moral ills that afflict humanity, including hunger, neglect, unemployment, and despair. There are many in your own midst.

Large concentrations of people create special problems and special needs. The personal effort and loyal collaboration of everybody are needed to find the right solutions, so that all men, women, and children can live in dignity and develop to the full their potential without having to suffer for lack of education, housing, employment, and cultural opportunities. Above all, a city needs a soul if it is to become a true home for human beings. You, the people, must give it this soul. And how do you do this? By loving each other. Love for each other must be the hallmark of your lives. In the Gospel Jesus Christ tells us, "You shall love your neighbor as yourself." This commandment of the Lord must by your inspiration in forming the human relationships among yourselves, so that nobody will ever feel alone or unwanted, or much less, rejected, despised, or hated.

Christ came with a message of joy to the poor. Human-Christian values are fostered when every effort is made so that no child anywhere in the world faces death because of lack of food, or faces a diminished intellectual and physical potential for want of sufficient nourishment, or has to bear all through life the scars of deprivation.

Much remains to be done to support those whose lives are wounded and to restore hope to those who are afraid of life. Courage is needed to resist pressures and false slogans, to proclaim the supreme dignity of all life, and to demand that society itself give it its protection. A distinguished American, Thomas Jefferson, once stated, "The care of human life and happiness and not their destruction is the just and only legitimate object of good government." I wish therefore to praise all the members of the Catholic Church and other Christian Churches, all men and women of the Judeo-Christian heritage, as well as all people of goodwill who unite in common dedication for the defense of life in its fullness and for the promotion of all human rights.

The poor of the world are your brothers and sisters in Christ. You must never be content to leave them just the crumbs from the feast. You must take of your substance, and not just of your abundance, in order to help them. And you must treat them like guests at your family table.

Once there was a rich man who dressed in purple and linen and feasted splendidly every day. At his gate lay a beggar named Lazarus, who was covered with sores. Lazarus longed to eat the scraps that fell from the rich man's table. Both the rich man and the beggar died and were carried before Abraham, and there judgment was rendered on their conduct. And the Scripture tells us that Lazarus found consolation, but that the rich man found torment. Was the rich man condemned because he had riches, because he abounded in earthly possessions, because he dressed in purple and linen and feasted splendidly every day? No, I would say that it was not for this reason. The rich man was condemned because he did not pay attention to the other man. Because he failed to take notice of Lazarus, the person who sat at his door and who longed to eat the scraps from his table. Nowhere does Christ condemn the mere possession of earthly goods as such. Instead, he pronounces very harsh words against those who use their possessions in a selfish way, without paying attention to the needs of others. The Sermon on the Mount begins with the words, "Blessed are the poor in spirit." And at the end of the account of the Last Judgment as found in St. Matthew's Gospel, Jesus speaks the words that we all know so well: "I was hungry and you gave me no food. I was thirsty and you gave me no drink. I was away from home and you gave me no welcome, naked and you gave me no clothing. I was ill and in prison and you did not come and comfort me."

The parable of the rich man and Lazarus must always be present in our memory; it must form our conscience. Christ demands openness from the rich, the affluent, the economically advanced; openness to the poor, the underdeveloped, and the disadvantaged. Christ demands an openness that is more than benign attention, more than token actions or halfhearted efforts that leave the poor as destitute as before, or even more so.

All of humanity must think of the parable of the rich man and the beggar. Humanity must translate into contemporary terms, in terms of economy and politics, in terms of all human rights, in terms of relations between the "first," "second," and "third world." We cannot stand idly by when thousands of human beings are dying of hunger. Nor can we remain indifferent when the rights of the human spirit are trampled upon, when violence is done to the human conscience in matters of truth, religion, and cultural creativity.

We cannot stand idly by, enjoying our own riches and freedom, if, in any place, the Lazarus of the twentieth century stands at our doors. In the light of the parable of Christ, riches and freedom mean a special responsibility. Riches and freedom create a special obligation. And so, in the name of the solidarity that binds us all together in a common humanity, I again proclaim the dignity of every human person; the rich man and Lazarus are both human beings, both of them equally created in the image and likeness of God, both of them equally redeemed by Christ, at a great price, the price of "the precious blood of Christ."

Brothers and sisters in Christ, with deep conviction and affection I repeat to you the words that I addressed to the world when I took up my apostolic ministry in the service of all men and women: "Do not be afraid. Open wide the doors for Christ. To his saving power open the bondaries of states and political systems, the vast fields of culture, civilization, and development. Do not be afraid. Christ knows what is in us. He alone knows it."

SUFFERING

You have not suffered in vain, for pain matures you in spirit, purifies you in heart, gives you a real sense of the world and of life, enriches you with goodness, patience, and endurance, gives you a sensation of deep peace, perfect joy, and happy hope.

Thinking of you, and of all those who are ill, I see a deep and mysterious analogy between your situation and that of the newborn Jesus in the manger at

Bethlehem: that baby was a little, frail, weak being, in need of everything, depending on everyone; yet he was the Son of God, the eternal Word incarnate in time, the Savior of mankind, the Lord of history.

How often you may have felt useless in your infirmity, a burden to your dear ones. You have experienced the humiliation, so deeply human, of being obliged to need others in everything, of being almost at the mercy of others. Look at Jesus in the cave at Bethlehem, who assures you that it is the world which needs the immeasurable riches of your suffering for its purification and for its growth.

Take heart! God loves you, because he sees in you the image of his Son suffering on earth! Your dear ones love you, because you are their flesh and blood! The Church loves you, because you enrich the treasure of the communion of saints! The Pope has a particular preference for you, because you are his most sensitive sons, and asks you for the help and strength of your apparent weakness, of your prayers and your sacrifices.

The Gospels are filled with instances where our Lord shows his particular love and concern for the sick and for all those in pain. Jesus loves those who suffered, and this attitude has been passed on to his Church. To love the sick is something that the Church has learned from Christ.

By his suffering and death Jesus took on himself all human suffering, and he gave it a new value. As a matter of fact, he calls upon the sick, upon everyone who suffers, to collaborate with him in the salvation of the world. Because of this, pain and sorrow are not endured alone or in vain. Although it remains difficult to understand suffering, Jesus has made it clear that its value is linked to his own suffering and death, to his own sacrifice. In other words, by your suffering you help Jesus in his work of salvation. This great truth is difficult to express accurately, but St. Paul puts it this way: "In my flesh I complete what is lacking in Christ's afflictions for the sake of his body, that is, the Church."

Your call to suffering requires strong faith and patience. It means you are called to love with a special intensity.

For two reasons, you are in a very special way my brothers and sisters: because of the love of Christ that binds us together, and, particularly, because you share so profoundly in the Mystery of the Cross and the Redemption of Jesus.

Thank you for the suffering you bear in your bodies and your hearts. Thank you for your example of acceptance, of patience, and of union with the suffering Christ. Thank you for filling up "what is lacking in the suffering of Christ for the sake of his body, the Church." May the peace and the joy of the Lord Jesus be always with you.

Cheer up, God is with you. You suffer, it is true, but he is near you. Trust in him, as you would trust in your own father.

If he has let you suffer, it is because he sees something good in it which today you do not yet know.

Your peace of mind is in your trust in God, who can never let you down.

Your call to suffering requires strong faith and patience. It means you are called to love with a special intensity.

We must never forget those who pay for their faith through condemnation, discrimination, suffering—even death. Their suffering is similar to Christ's before the ancient tribunal of Pontius Pilate.

Live your life in awareness of Easter.

It is difficult sometimes to see light beyond the darkness but the Christian is he who at night waits trustfully for the smile of dawn, he who through the darkness and sorrow of Good Friday sees the glory and the joy of Easter Sunday. Christ rose again and therefore his word is divine: God loves us, man is saved, history is redeemed.

The crucified Christ rose from the tomb and brought hope to humanity. Death has its limits. Christ opened a great hope—the hope of life beyond the sphere of death. Years, centuries have gone by and the struggle between evil and good, sin and grace goes on. We should think with uneasiness about where the modern world is directing itself.

Yet, Paschal Lamb, even if in the history of man—of individuals, families, societies, and, indeed, all humanity—evil has developed disproportionately, eclipsing the horizon of good, nonetheless it will not overpower you. Death will no longer strike you even if in the history of man and in the time in which we live evil would increase its power, even if the powers of darkness and the forces of evil would rage, you, Paschal Victim, have already scored the victory, and you have made it our victory. Evil will never be reconciled with good, so let us celebrate today the resurrection. The mystery of the resurrection remains in the heart of the multitudes, in the very heart of the innumerable multitudes of nations, languages, races, cultures, and religions. The Paschal Mystery remains deep in the heart of our world and from there no one can remove it.

JOY

Christ came to bring joy: joy to children, joy to parents, joy to families and to friends, joy to workers and to scholars, joy to the sick and to the elderly, joy to all humanity. In a true sense, joy is the keynote of the Christian message and the recurring motif of the gospels. Recall the first words of the angel to Mary: "Rejoice, O full of grace, the Lord is with you." And at the birth of Jesus, the angels announced to the shepherds: "Listen, I bring you news of great joy, joy to be shared by all people." Years later, as Jesus entered Jerusalem riding on a colt, the whole group of disciples joyfully began to praise God at the top of their voices. "Blessed is the King who comes in the name of the Lord!" We are told that some Pharisees in the crowd complained, saying, "Master, stop your disciples." But Jesus answered, "I tell you, if they were silent, the very stones would cry out."

Are not those words of Jesus still true today? If we are silent about the joy that comes from knowing Jesus, the very stones of our cities will cry out! For we are an Easter people and "Alleluia" is our song. With St. Paul I exhort you: "Rejoice in the Lord always. I say it again, rejoice."

Rejoice because Jesus has come into the world!

*Rejoice because Jesus has died upon
the cross!*

*Rejoice because he rose again from
the dead!*

*Rejoice because in baptism, he washed
away our sins!*

*Rejoice because Jesus has come to set
us free!*

*And rejoice because he is the master
of our life!*

But how many people have never
known this joy? They feed on emptiness
and tread the paths of despair. They
walk in darkness and the shadow of
death. And we need not look to the far
ends of the earth for them. They live in
our neighborhoods, they walk down our
streets, they may even be members of
our own families. They live without true
joy because they live without hope. They
have never heard, really heard, the Good

News of Jesus Christ, because they have never met a brother or a sister who touched their lives with the love of Jesus and lifted them up from their misery.

We must go to them therefore as messengers of hope. We must bring to them the witness of true joy. We must pledge to them our commitment to work for a just society and city where they feel respected and loved.

And so I encourage you, be men and women of deep and abiding faith. Be heralds of hope. Be messengers of joy. Be true workers for justice. Let the Good News of Christ radiate from your hearts, and the peace he alone gives remain forever in your souls.

I want you to be happy, always happy in the Lord; I repeat, what I want is your happiness. There is no need to worry; but if there is anything you need, pray for it, asking God for it with prayer and thanksgiving, and that peace of God which is so much greater than we can understand, will guard your hearts and your thoughts, in Christ Jesus.

LOVE

We must love one another with a pure heart fervently; we must bear one another's burdens: these simple words explain so much of the meaning of life.

I propose to you the option of love, which is the opposite of escape. If you really accept that love from Christ, it will lead you to God. Perhaps in the priesthood or religious life, perhaps in some special service to your brothers and sisters, especially to the needy, the poor, the lonely, the abandoned, those whose rights have been trampled upon, or those whose basic needs have not been provided for. Whatever you make of your life, let it be something that reflects the love of Christ. The whole People of God will be all the richer because of the diversity of your commitments. In whatever you do, remember that Christ is calling you, in one way or another, to the service of love: the love of God and of your neighbor.

Real love is demanding. I would fail in my mission if I did not clearly tell you so. For it was Jesus, Jesus himself, who said, "You are my friends if you do what I command you." Love demands effort and a personal commitment to the will of God. It means discipline and sacrifice, but it also means joy and human fulfillment.

The absolute and gentle authority of the Lord answers to the most profound feelings in man, to the noblest aspirations of his mind, his will, and his heart. That authority does not express itself in the exercise of power, but in love and truth.

We cannot live without love. If we do not encounter love, if we do not experience it and make it our own, and if we do not participate intimately in it, our life is meaningless.

Without love we remain incomprehensible to ourselves. Thus, everyone of you needs a vibrant relationship of love to the Lord, a profound loving union with Christ.

Charity. Love. The foundation and fullness of God's glory in man and man's glory in God. "Charity is patient and kind. Charity is not envious; it does not boast or grow conceited; it is not rude or self-indulgent; it does not take offense or bear any grudge; it takes no pleasure in injustice but rejoices in the truth. It excuses all things, believes all things, hopes all things, and endures all things. Charity will never end."

Jesus left us love as his commandment. Love was to be the mainstay and the prop of the spiritual identity of his disciples as they confronted the hatred which at various times and in various forms was to be hurled at them by the world: "If the world hates you, know that before hating you it hated Me."

There are two commandments of love, as the Master expressly states, but there is only one love. One and the same love embraces God and one's neighbor: God above everything because he is above everything; one's neighbor with the measure of man, and so "as oneself." These two loves are so closely connected with each other that one cannot exist without the other. It is not possible, therefore, to separate one love from the other.

True love of one's neighbor, for the very reason that it is true love, is at the same time, love of God. Some people may be astonished by this. It is certainly astonishing.

When the Lord Jesus presents to his listeners the vision of the Last Judgment, he says, "I was hungry and you gave me food, I was thirsty and you gave me drink." Those who listen to these words are surprised for we hear them ask: "Lord, when did we see you hungry and feed you?" And the answer is: "I tell you solemnly, insofar as you did this to one of the least of these brothers, you did it to me."

Love is the force that opens hearts to the word of Jesus and to his Redemption; love is the only basis of human relationships that respect in one another the dignity of the children of God created in his image and saved by the death and resurrection of Jesus; love is the only driving force that impels us to share with our brothers and sisters all that we are and have.

Every human—and the whole of humanity—lives between love and hatred. If you do not accept love, hatred will creep into your heart with ease and begin to fill it more and more, bearing more and more poisonous fruits.

Love is the power that gives rise to dialogue, in which we listen to each other and learn from each other. Love gives rise, above all, to the dialogue of prayer in which we listen to God's word, which is alive in the Holy Bible and alive in the life of the Church. Let love then build the bridges across our differences and, at times, our contrasting positions.

UNITY

∾

There is a word that must be part of the vocabulary of every Christian, especially when barriers of hate and mistrust have been constructed. This word is reconciliation. "So if you are offering your gift at the altar, and there remember that your brother has something against you, leave your gift there before the altar and go; be reconciled with your brother, and then come and offer your gift." This command of Jesus is stronger than any barrier that human inadequacy or malice can build. Even when our belief in the fundamental goodness of every human being has been shaken or undermined, even if long-held convictions and attitudes have hardened our hearts, there is one source of power that is stronger than every disappointment, bitterness, or ingrained mistrust, and that power is Jesus Christ, who brought forgiveness and reconciliation to the world.

The great promise contained in the Gospel is truly encouraging and uplifting: "For where two or three are gathered in my name, there am I in the midst of them." And so we rejoice exceedingly to know that Jesus Christ is with us.

We know that he is near to us with the power of his Paschal Mystery, and that from his Paschal Mystery we draw light and strength to walk in what St. Paul calls "the newness of life."

What a great grace it is for the entire Christian world, that, in this our day, the Holy Spirit has powerfully stirred up in human hearts a real desire for this "newness of life." And what a great gift of God it is that there exists today among Christians a deeper realization of the need to be perfectly one in Christ and in his Church; to be one, in accordance with Christ's own prayer, even as he and his Father are one.

Our desire for Christian unity springs from a need to be faithful to the will of God, as revealed in Christ. Our unity in Christ, moreover, conditions the effectiveness of our evangelization: it determines the credibility of our witness before the world. Christ prayed for the unity of his disciples, precisely "so that the world may believe . . . ."

The work of reconciliation, the road to unity, may be long and difficult. But, as on the way to Emmaus, the Lord himself is with us on the way, always making "as if to go on." He will stay with us until the longed-for moment comes, when we can join together in recognizing him in the Holy Scriptures and in the breaking of the bread.

Meanwhile, the internal renewal of the Catholic Church, in total fidelity to the Second Vatican Council, to which I pledged all my energies at the beginning of my papal ministry, must continue with undiminished vigor. This renewal is itself an indispensable contribution to the work of unity between Christians. As we each in our respective Churches grow in our searching of the Holy Scriptures, in our fidelity to and continuity with the age-old tradition of the Christian

Church, in our search for holiness and for authenticity of Christian living, we shall also be coming closer to Christ, and therefore closer to one another in Christ.

It is he alone, through the action of his Holy Spirit, who can bring our hopes to fulfillment. In him we place all our trust; in "Jesus Christ our hope." Despite our human weakness and our sins, despite all obstacles, we accept in humility and faith the great principle enunciated by our Savior. "What is impossible with men is possible with God."

Much has been accomplished, but there is still much to be done. We must go forward, however, with a spirit of hope. Even the very desire for the complete unity in faith—which is lacking between us, and which must be achieved before we can lovingly celebrate the Eucharist together in truth—is itself a gift of the Holy Spirit, for which we offer humble praise to God. We are confident that through our common prayer the Lord Jesus will lead us, at a moment dependent on the sovereign action of his Holy Spirit, to the fullness of ecclesial unity.

Faithfulness to the Holy Spirit calls for interior conversion and fervent prayer. In the words of the Second Vatican Council: "This change of heart and holiness of life, along with public and private prayer for the unity of Christians, should be regarded as the soul of the whole ecumenical movement. . . ." It is important that every individual Christian search his or her heart to see what may obstruct the attainment of full union among Christians. And let us pray that the genuine need for the patience to await God's hour will never occasion complacency in the status quo of division in faith. By divine grace may the need for patience never become a substitute for the definitive and generous response which God asks that there be given to his invitation to perfect unity in Christ.

We must all be ministers of reconciliation. We must by example as well as by word try to move citizens, communities, and politicians towards the ways of tolerance, cooperation, and love. No fear of criticism, no risk of resentment, must deter us from this task. The charity of Christ compels us. Precisely because we have one Lord, Jesus Christ, we must accept together the responsibility of the vocation we have received from him.

Dear brothers, with a conviction linked to our faith, we realize that the destiny of the world is at stake, because the credibility of the Gospel has been challenged. Only in perfect unity can we Christians adequately give witness to the truth. And so our fidelity to Jesus Christ urges us to do more, to pray more, to love more.

May Christ the Good Shepherd show us how to lead our people along the path of love to the goal of perfect unity for the praise and glory of the Father, and of the Son, and of the Holy Spirit. Amen.

A
MESSAGE
OF HOPE

∽

I come to you in the name of Jesus Christ, who died in order "to gather into one the children of God who are scattered abroad." This is my mission, my message to you: Jesus Christ who is our peace. Christ is our peace. And today and forever he repeats to us, "My peace I give to you, my peace I leave with you."

Never before in the history of mankind has peace been so much talked about and so ardently desired as in our day. The growing interdependence of peoples and nations makes almost everyone subscribe, at least in principle, to the ideal of universal human brotherhood. Great international institutions debate humanity's peaceful co-existence. Public opinion is growing in consciousness of the absurdity of war as a means to resolve differences. More and more, peace is seen as a necessary condition for fraternal relations among nations, and among peoples. Peace is more and more clearly seen as the only way to justice; peace is itself the work of justice. And yet, again and again, one can see how peace is undermined and destroyed. Why is it then that our convictions do not always match our behavior and our attitudes? Why is it that we do not seem to be able to banish all conflicts from our lives?

Peace is the result of many converging attitudes and realities; it is the product of moral concerns of ethical principles based on the Gospel message and fortified by it.

"Man does not live on bread alone"— we are not only hungry for bread, we are hungry, perhaps even more, for truth. We are hungry for freedom, when some of our fundamental rights are violated, such as the right to freedom of conscience and to religious freedom, the right to the education of children in conformity with the faith and convictions of parents and families, the right to instruction according to ability and not according to some political situation or a vision of the world imposed by force.

Truth, the power of peace! Let us join together in strengthening peace through the resources of peace itself. The primary resource is truth, for it is preeminently truth radiating its light without restriction that constitutes the serene and powerful divining face of peace.

I appeal to all who love freedom and justice to give a chance to all in need, to the poor, and to the powerless. Break open the hopeless cycles of poverty and ignorance that are still the lot of too many of our brothers and sisters; the hopeless cycles of prejudice that linger on despite enormous progress toward effective equality in education and employment; the cycles of despair in which are imprisoned all those that lack decent food, shelter, or employment; the cycles

of underdevelopment that are the conse-
quence of international mechanisms that
subordinate the human existence to the
domination of partially conceived economic progress; and finally, the inhuman
cycles of war that spring from the violation of man's fundamental rights and
produce still graver violation of them.

I proclaim, with the conviction of my
faith in Christ and with an awareness of
my mission, that violence is evil, that violence is unacceptable as a solution to
problems, that violence is unworthy of
humans.

Violence is a lie, for it goes against the
truth of our faith, the truth of our humanity. Violence destroys what it claims to
defend: the dignity, the life, the freedom
of human beings. Violence is a crime

against humanity, for it destroys the very fabric of society.

Let us remember that the word remains forever: "All who take the sword will perish by the sword."

Do not reject Christ, you who are the builders of the human world. Do not reject him, you who, in whatever way and in whatever sphere, are building the world of today and of tomorrow, the world of culture and civilization, the world of economics and of politics, the world of science and information. You who are building the world of order ... or of terror? Do not refuse Christ, for he is the cornerstone.

It is worth dedicating oneself to the cause of Christ, who wants valiant and decided hearts; it is worth devoting oneself to another for Christ, in order to bring him on his way to eternity; it is worth making an option for an ideal that will give you great joys, even if at the same time it demands a good many sacrifices. The Lord does not abandon his followers.

"Deliver us from evil!" Reciting these words of Christ's prayer, it is difficult to interpret them in any way which does not differ from that which opposes peace, that which destroys it, that which threatens it. And so let us pray, "Deliver us from war, from hatred, from the destruction of human lives! Do not allow us to kill! Do not allow the use of those means that serve death and destruction and whose power, range of action, and accuracy go beyond the limits hitherto known."

Do not allow them to be used ever!

"Deliver us from evil!" Defend us from war! From any war, Father who art in heaven. Father of life and giver of peace, the Pope, the son of a nation that, during its history and particularly in our century, has been among those most sorely tried in the horror, the cruelty, and the cataclysm of war, beseeches you. He beseeches you for all the peoples in the world, for all countries, and for all continents. He beseeches you in the name of Christ, the Prince of Peace.

Hiroshima 26 February, 1981

Hear my voice, for it is the voice of the victims of all wars and violence among individuals and nations.

Hear my voice, for it is the voice of all children who suffer when people put their faith in weapons and war.

Hear my voice, when I beg you to instill into the hearts of all human beings the wisdom of peace, the strength of justice, and the joy of fellowship.

Hear my voice, for I speak for the multitudes in every period of history who do not want war and are ready to walk the road to peace.

Hear my voice and grant insight and strength so that we may always respond to hatred with love, to injustice with total dedication to justice, to need with the sharing of self, to war with peace.

The message which I wish to leave with you is a message of certitude and hope, the certitude that peace is possible when it is based on the recognition of the fatherhood of God and the brotherhood of all men; the hope that the sense of moral responsibility which every person must assume will make it possible to create a better world in freedom, in justice, and in love.

"Peace be with you!" These were the first words that Jesus spoke to his apostles after his resurrection. With these words the risen Christ restored peace to their hearts, at a time when they were still in a state of shock after the first terrible experience of Good Friday. Tonight, in the name of our Lord Jesus Christ, in the power of his Spirit, in the midst of a world that is anxious about its own existence, I repeat these words to you, for they are words of life: "Peace be with you!"

Jesus does not merely give us peace. He gives us his peace accompanied by his justice. He *is* peace and justice. He becomes our peace and our justice.

What does this mean? It means that Jesus Christ—the Son of God made man, the perfect man—perfects, restores, and manifests in himself the unsurpassable dignity that God wishes to give to us from the beginning. He is the one who realizes in himself what we have the vocation to be: fully reconciled with the Father, fully one in ourselves, fully devoted to others. Jesus Christ is living peace and living justice.

Jesus Christ makes us sharers in what he is. Through his incarnation, the Son of God in a certain manner united himself with every human being. In our inmost being he has recreated us; in our inmost being he has reconciled us with ourselves, reconciled us with our brothers and sisters; he is our peace.

"Peace I leave with you, my peace I give to you." My constant prayer for all of you is this: that there may be peace in justice and in love. May the praying

voice of all those who believe in God—
Christians and non-Christians alike—
bring it about that the moral resources
present in the hearts of men and women
of goodwill be united for the common
good, and call down from heaven that
peace which human efforts alone cannot
effect.